EXPERIENCING
GOD

Thomas Green, S.J., was one of the most beloved and most accessible of all modern Catholic spiritual writers. *Experiencing God* is classic Green: clear, concise, based on years of experience as a believer and a spiritual director, and enormously helpful for anyone seeking to move closer to God in prayer and daily life. Highly recommended.

James Martin, S.J.
Author of *My Life with the Saints*

Experiencing God offers a very readable synthesis of Thomas Green's own thinking on prayer. I found the book to be very helpful, because it's not just about stages of a person's prayer life but about spiritual growth itself: from knowing to loving God, from loving to truly loving God. I would recommend the book to anyone committed to a life-long encounter with God, as well as to spiritual directors, prayer companions, and pastors, who must from time to time find words to articulate how to move forward in that mysterious reality we call prayer.

Michael McCarthy, S.J.
Assistant Professor
Santa Clara University

EXPERIENCING
GOD

The Three Stages of Prayer

THOMAS H. GREEN, S.J.

ave maria press AmP **notre dame, indiana**

www.avemariapress.com

ISBN-10 1-59471-245-X   ISBN-13 978-1-59471-245-6

Cover image © Jupiter Unlimited.

Cover and text design by Katherine Robinson Coleman.

Printed and bound in the United States of America.

Library of Congress Cataloging-in-Publication Data

Green, Thomas H. (Thomas Henry), 1932-2009
  Experiencing God : the three stages of prayer / Thomas H. Green.
       p. cm.
  ISBN-13: 978-1-59471-245-6 (pbk.)
  ISBN-10: 1-59471-245-X (pbk.)
  1. Prayer--Catholic Church. 2. Contemplation. I. Title.
  BV210.3.G728 2010
  242'.802--dc22

                                             2009049531

CONTENTS

FOREWORD

When I woke up on the morning of March 14, 2009, I was shocked to discover—from Facebook updates, of all things—that Fr. Tom Green had passed away. I had known that he was sick, but the suddenness of his passing still came as a sad surprise.

Soon after I had sent my condolences, the present rector of San Jose Seminary, Vic de Jesus, kindly called me up long distance to inform me of the details of Tom's passing: how Tom had come home from the hospital the night before; how one of the seminarians had peeked into his room that morning and found him sitting in his chair, with his pipe on his chest. He went very quickly, which was a real mercy.

I first met Tom Green thirty years ago. In my senior year at the Ateneo, school year 1979–80, I was in Fr. Green's philosophy of language class. It was a wonderful course, and, thirty years later, the fact that I can still remember so much—of the logical positivists, of Wittgenstein, that language is inescapably metaphorical, that some concepts are essentially contested—is surely testimony to the outstanding clarity and excellence of Fr. Green's teaching.

My second encounter with Fr. Green was through his books. *Opening to God*, which I read twice—once as a college student and, more seriously, as a novice in the society—was a deeply influential book in my life. I don't think it is an exaggeration to say that it taught me how to pray. I read all his other books too, but my personal favorite, the book which I think is his best and wisest, is *When the Wells Run Dry*.

Two key insights from that book have remained with me through the decades. The first insight is that darkness happens, not just in prayer but in life, to move us, in his words, from "loving to truly loving." I still recall, more or less accurately, a sentence from the book in which he reflects on a married couple's promise to love each other "for better or worse": "The better, the good times are there to teach us the joy of loving; the worse happens to teach us to love truly."

The second insight is at the end of the book, when Fr. Green uses the image of floating (as contrasted with swimming) as a metaphor for the mature life of faith. You give up control over your life ("swimming"); you remain active (otherwise you would sink) but allow yourself to be led; you let go and entrust yourself to the unpredictable flow of the sea of love that surrounds you, and you let it take you where it wills.

My third and most lasting encounter with Fr. Green lasted from 1996 to 2004, when we lived together in the same community and worked on the same formation team in San Jose Seminary. At that time we were also co-faculty members of Loyola School of Theology. From 2000 to 2004, the years I served as rector of San Jose, Fr. Green was my vice-rector. He had the room directly above mine.

For eight years, we shared meals and attended many staff meetings together. With the rest of the Jesuit team, we processed hundreds of applications to the seminary, sat through hours of evaluations of seminarians, discussed and occasionally argued over seminary policies. Almost every Monday evening for eight years we had common prayer together in the BVM chapel on the third floor of San Jose, and, after prayer, shared a special meal in the Jesuit community recreation room.

When you live that long with another Jesuit, you get to know him quite well. I got to know about Tom's legendary regularity of life. He followed the same schedule or "cycle" almost every day, every week, every year. If it was 1:30 p.m., he could invariably be found in his rocking chair on the fifth floor reading the papers. If it was the third (I forget which, actually) Sunday of the month, he would have Mass in Balara or for the L'Arche community. If it was summer vacation, then he would be giving a retreat somewhere in the United States. And woe to you if you moved that rocking chair, as one unwitting minister did!

I remember pleasant and witty Jesuit banter with Tom during meals. Once, Roque Ferriols was talking about Jesuit Bishop Honesto "Onie" Pacana and kept referring to him as "Honey Pacana." The rest of us—Art Borja was there, I remember—corrected Fr. Roque and told him that the bishop's nickname was pronounced "Onie" not "Honey." When Roque said that he had always thought the bishop's nickname was "Honey," Tom Green quipped in a deadpan way: "Oh, I thought you were just close." That brought the house down.

Tom was not perfect, I discovered. (His devoted lay friends, "the Golden Girls," who took such good care of him, also knew that.) He tended to want things his way. He got cross and cranky when things did not go the way he wanted them to go. He could express his opinions a bit too dogmatically. He did not admit his mistakes easily.

And yet, I appreciated his presence in the community and on the seminary formation team. He was a very generous (he had so many directees!) and wise spiritual director. He was a man of very good and balanced judgment where people were concerned, and I always valued his perceptions of applicants or seminarians. When I consulted him as vice-rector on issues of the seminary, I usually received very sensible counsel.

By the time I got to San Jose, Tom was a grandfather figure to the seminarians. His cheerful and easy manner of dealing with them and the personal witness he gave of a man who had grown old—and happily so—in the priesthood was something, I think, of inestimable value for San Jose. Having been part of San Jose for over three decades, he had become for generations of "Josefinos" an icon, a living link between the past and the present, a symbol of their happy years in the seminary. With Tom's passing away, an era in the history of San Jose came to an end—Tom was a presence that cannot be replaced. In all my years as rector and as provincial, Tom always told me that he hoped he could die in San Jose. He got his wish. I am glad for him. Now, I trust that he is in the presence of the One whom he wrote about, spoke about, and served so faithfully and generously for so many years. Now, I trust the

darkness has become light for him, and, with a joy no
words can describe, he can let go and, at last, float.

Rev. Daniel P. Huang, S.J.
Philippine Society of Jesus

PART ONE:

GETTING TO KNOW
GOD

I would like, in the first part of this book, to say something about the fundamental idea of prayer. The background comes from something I wrote about in *Opening to God*. I began *Opening to God* by asking, "What is prayer?" I responded by saying that we can define prayer as the opening of the mind and the heart to God; I added that we can also define prayer as a personal encounter with God in love. Both of these definitions have a certain value, and I will still stick by them as basic ideas.

PRAYER: AN OPENING AND AN ENCOUNTER

P rayer as the opening of the mind and heart to God involves not only the head, but the heart, not only the understanding, but the affective side of a person, the emotions, and the will; that prayer is not primarily a lifting, as the old catechism definition said, but an opening. This first definition of prayer, an opening of the mind and heart to God, is helpful in terms of clarifying what one might call the "faculties" involved in the basic approach to prayer. It is the more abstract and descriptive of the two definitions.

The second definition, a personal encounter with God in love, is really the one I prefer, as it is the more experiential of the two—it is the one I would ultimately want to base things on as a spiritual director. But one of the things I have learned is that the second definition, while more experiential and (I think) more personal, can be rather discouraging to people when God seems absent. If we describe prayer as a personal encounter with God in love, then when people get into dryness, they are tempted to feel that they're not praying because there's no encounter.

This is a problem that will need to be addressed later in the book, but I mention it now mainly to indicate that both definitions of prayer have their value. If my prayer has run into dryness, I might well be more encouraged by the first definition. In this case, even though I cannot see that I am encountering God, I am open, mind and heart. I don't see what's happening. I cannot pinpoint that this is an encounter; in fact, it seems to me that God is absent. I can check whether I am truly open, in both mind and heart, to God. If so, I'm praying. In that case, I think, the first definition would be more reassuring. The disadvantage of the first definition is that it focuses more on what we do, whereas the second one focuses on the fact that prayer is an encounter—an *encuentro*—between persons. Prayer experience is not something that I do alone. Rather, it is the interaction between God and me.

THE REAL BEGINNING:
VOCAL PRAYER

At the same time, reflecting on prayer as the years have passed, I think one good observation is that the above definitions elucidate what prayer *should be*, rather than what prayer in fact often *is*—at least at the very beginning. That is, I think it might be a little more experiential and honest to start from the reality that for most people, prayer is not like these two definitions. For most people, even to get into a mentality resonant with these definitions can involve some real effort, some real frustration, and even some discouragement. The process can take much of their lives. So it might be good to start by recognizing that for most people prayer is neither an opening nor an encounter. Prayer for most means vocal prayer. I really think that's what most people, in their real life experience, would understand prayer to be.

I've had some very interesting experiences as a result of writing books on prayer. One thing that has been quite striking for me is the privilege I've had of directing two Protestant ministers. Both of them come from traditions very different from my own— they come from the Methodist and Presbyterian traditions. One works here in the Philippines, and is an American who is here as a sort of missionary, running a church for expatriates in Makati; the other is from Australia, a female minister, who has worked her whole ordained life in Australia. It has been quite striking that both of them have said to me that, in their traditions, prayer does not normally mean listening. It was quite a revelation to me that, in Protestant traditions, at least the ones from which they came, there was a good deal of focus on prayer as asking, prayer as petition, and prayer as adoration, but not so much on prayer as personal encounter. I think that's why, when they read my books, they were somehow drawn to seek me out, because they seemed to feel they had found something which perhaps was lacking in their own traditions.

I balance that story about my Protestant directees by mentioning that I have been working with two prayer groups in different Catholic parishes here in Manila. We've been meeting about once a month for the past year or so, and in both groups people have been saying that our monthly sharing about prayer and the little assignments I have given them in the intervening weeks have completely revolutionized their experience of prayer. I was happy to hear that but a bit surprised that it was that revolutionary for them. What was "revolutionary" really ended up being the same point as the one my Protestant directees had made.

᾽ As one woman said, she had been raised in the convent schools to identify prayer with asking and with novenas and with reading from the prayer books. She put it very beautifully—this is a woman who has grown children, so she's not so young—saying that all of her life she's been prayerful, but she was lost without the book. Unless she had a prayer book there to read, she didn't know what to do. She said for the first time in her life, when we began to share in these groups, she has found herself putting the prayer book aside, beginning to suspect that maybe it was better to just listen to the Lord and to be more spontaneous with him. She was surprised that she could survive without the crutch of the prayer book, and even more surprised that she finds now she's reluctant to pick up the prayer book. She thinks that she's now found something better.

In short, my experience has led me to the realization that my Protestant friends' experiences are quite valid for most Catholics, too. Many other people have confirmed this experience. It seems to boil down to two important points about most people's prayer: that there is something better, yes, but also that most of us, Catholic or Protestant, did not know that there was something better. For most people, prayer means vocal prayer, and that in turn means talking to God. And talking to God very frequently means using somebody else's words. Reading the old Vatican II missal put out by the Daughters of St. Paul, you find a daily meditation in which Father Alberione's words or the words of Pope Paul VI or somebody else are given to us, precooked, for our reflection. That has been very much our tradition—I pray by reading somebody else's words.

Now, in trying to wrestle with the issue of praying vocally, I would say that it is in fact a good way to pray. I'll say a word about the possibilities of growth in vocal prayer in a moment. But I will also ask, why might this not be the best way? To use an analogy: suppose a boy named Herman is courting a girl named Suzy-Bell. Herman is rather shy and somewhat tongue-tied. He doesn't know what to say to Suzy-Bell, so he gets a copy of Shakespeare's *Romeo and Juliet*. Then, as courtship goes here in the Philippines, he gets a guitar and plays under her balcony, and when she comes out on the balcony with stars in her eyes his heart begins to beat fast, and he takes out his copy of *Romeo and Juliet* and reads Romeo's words to Juliet. What would the girl think? Sure, Romeo's words are beautiful (especially if you know and love Shakespeare), but they are not the boy's. Suzy-Bell might then say to him, "Well, for heaven's sakes, Herman, speak for yourself! I'd like to hear from you!" Herman then replies, "Yes, but Shakespeare speaks much better than I do." She responds, "Well, fine, but I'm not marrying Shakespeare!"

Now that's the problem, I think, with vocal prayer. Vocal prayer is somebody else's words, which can be a help to start, but sooner or later the Lord, like the girl, is going to say to us, "For heaven's sakes, speak for yourself! Stop reading me somebody else's words and let's begin communicating ourselves." Now, we may be shy with God, we may be insecure, that's true, and someone else's words may help us as a start. But Herman's own words to Suzy-Bell are far better, even if they're not very good English. They are far better than Shakespeare's words to express what's going on between him and her. Does that make sense? I think that it's very important that Herman and Suzy-Bell find the words to express their own love and their own experience. In addition, Herman has to learn to listen and not just talk. The danger with vocal prayer is that we end up doing all the talking. So there are two dangers, really: first, we end up using precooked words that are not our own; second, we end up doing all the talking.

Having critiqued vocal prayer, let me say something positive about it. St. Teresa of Avila is the great authority here. She wrote her *Way of Perfection* when her sisters asked her to teach them how to pray. The main reason *Way of Perfection* exists is because in Teresa's day women were not educated; they did not have much schooling. Even Teresa herself was educated in something more like a finishing school than a formal university. Most of Teresa's sisters could not read, and printing was just beginning in those days. For most of them, vocal prayer was what they knew, and the shorter and the more simple the prayers were, the more likely the sisters were to know them.

The point of St. Teresa's *Way of Perfection* is that one can reach the heights of contemplation even through vocal prayer. I think it's a great book for people who feel that some of the things I have discussed in other books are a bit too sophisticated for them. The *Way of Perfection* speaks to that problem. Vocal prayer can lead to the heights of contemplation, provided, as Teresa says, that we think about what we're saying. Teresa says that reciting vocal prayers without thinking is useless (or worse than useless) because it is, in a way, insulting to God. It is talking to God without thinking about what I am saying as if there were some magic in the words. Teresa says that if we think about what we're saying vocal prayer can lead us all the way to the heights of contemplation. I think that's very true.

ENCOUNTER IS NOT
A TECHNIQUE

Whether somebody has a strong foundation in modern exegesis, or whether someone has read all the latest spiritual books—these things won't make a pray-er out of him. They can help—they can be a great help for those who have the capacity for it, and normally God will demand it of those who have the capacity, in part because God doesn't want us to be lazy—but for those who don't have the capacity, if they simply think about what they are saying, they can go just as far. The simple squatter-area woman can go just as far as the most learned theologian, provided her prayer is more than just words.

Having discussed vocal prayer, I think we can now come back to our definition of prayer as an opening of the mind and heart to God. This opening can happen in different forms and at different levels of sophistication. At all of these levels, however, the core of the experience is *personal encounter*. Because of this, when people pray, very often the most difficult problem is learning to listen, learning to keep still. Using this definition, I talked in *Opening to God* about how, in a strict sense, there are no techniques of prayer. I still feel very strongly that this is the case.

As a matter of fact, I think that people are beginning to see that meditative practices like yoga, which can be a great help to coming to quiet, are not techniques for encountering God for the Christian. The basic point I made in *Opening to God* is that there can be no techniques for encountering God because God is not manipulable by us. God is the Lord of the encounter, so there's no way we can turn God on and off automatically. Praying is not just a question of getting the right posture or the right place or learning the right mantra. That would make it magical, and maybe it's good to say a further word about that. The point of magic is to manipulate God. That's why it's not good religion. Magic and superstition are attempts to get God under our control.

Even with things like novenas, I think, we can run into a problem in which there's a certain magical element to our prayer. I remember when I was young my mother saying (she was a bit of a freethinker for her time), "If I ever made a novena, I would make ten days or eight, not nine." And I remember that since the good sisters were training us in a more traditional way, we used to be scandalized by her. But her point was a very good one. She said, "I can't believe that for God there's magic in the number nine, that somehow I can get his ear if I do it nine times, but that he won't hear me if I do it eight or ten." There's a very good point there. I'm not against novenas, because if you're going to have some structure, somebody has to decide how many times you will pray. But it might be nice if somebody developed an eight-day novena, just to show that it doesn't have to be nine days, that God doesn't only hear nines, that he's also aware of eights and tens and elevens and sevens and so on.

Even in our devotions, we can lay much more stress on the numbers and finding the right technique. In our practice of indulgences, if you remember the ones that were given on All Saints Day (a practice that Pope Paul VI somewhat eliminated), people could get a plenary indulgence for every visit they made to the church, and you'd see the old people and sometimes not so old people standing in the doorway of the church with one foot in and one foot out. They would step in and say their required prayers and then out and then back in. They would have been much better off if they had settled down and encountered God in the church, but because of the supernatural bookkeeping which had come into our religion with the indulgences, they spent their whole day on the threshold of the church going in and out. This is a very good way to foster superstition, I think, but not a very good way to encounter God. What began as a practice to encourage people to make visits to church, which was a very good goal, somehow got distorted through bringing in the mystique of numbers.

My point is that there is no way to manipulate God. Nevertheless, people try. Simple people try through things like novenas and devotions. Sophisticated people try by joining the latest fad. Whether they are sophisticated or simple, very often what is in people's minds is, "how can I find the right way to turn God on?" One of the important points I tried to make in *Opening to God* is that there's really no way to turn God on. God is the Lord of the encounter.

GOOD WORKING
ORDER

S piritual directors do talk about techniques of prayer, however. They've talked about them through the whole history of the church. So what do we mean by *technique*? There must be some valid meaning there, and it's precisely that which I wish to explore next. I have in the past used the analogy of a radio to describe technique in prayer, and I've since found a way of expanding on that a bit. In the past, I talked about the radio as an instrument for listening to classical music or listening to a good religious broadcast or something like that. You could use the TV, but let's stick to the radio analogy for the moment. When I want to hear, let us say, classical music, the first thing I need is a good receiver. If I don't have a radio, or if the radio's not working, I'm not going to be able to hear the music no matter how well the station is broadcasting. No matter how beautiful the Daughters of St. Paul are doing their job, if I don't have a working receiver, it's not going to work for me.

Now, assuming I have a radio, the first thing I will need in order to hear well is quiet. And there are techniques of coming to quiet if I want to listen to the radio. If I'm listening to the music on the radio in my room, and somebody calls on the telephone (as they often do) and if the connection is not very good, as it often is not, sometimes I have trouble hearing them until I shut the radio off. I have to ask them to wait a minute while I go over and turn off the radio so I can hear them on the telephone. In order to listen to somebody on the phone, you have to get quiet. In order to listen to the radio, you have to get quiet.

The first thing we need in prayer, too, if we're going to hear God, is to come to quiet. That's where the radio analogy, I think, has its first application. I think all these techniques of yoga, Zen, and the Jesus Prayer can, at a basic level, bring us to quiet. "Nonprayerful" things like listening to good music, strolling, and so on can as well. As such, techniques of coming to quiet are valid. But notice, no matter how quiet I become, the quiet does not produce God. Techniques are not for *making* God speak. Rather, techniques are for coming to a listening attitude myself. It's still up to God whether to speak or not.

Once we are quiet, the second thing we have to look at is whether the "radio" is working. We need a radio that is in good condition and is properly tuned. And in prayer, that corresponds to techniques of purification. This is the way that we are the "radio receivers" in the encounter with God. The first question that has to be asked is, is there sufficient quiet to hear? The second is, is the receiver in good condition and are we tuned in? I use that analogy to point out that in a good prayer life, in addition to quiet, we also need a well-tuned and well-functioning receiver. This is where all of the techniques of purification come in. I've discussed in other works—too briefly, I think— the value of penance, the value of the Sacrament of Reconciliation (what used to be called the Sacrament of Penance), and the value of the examen of conscience as methods of purification. It might now be a good time to say a word or two more about penance, reconciliation, and the examen.

One of the reviewers of my book *Opening to God* raised the question, "Since the book is about how to pray, why does the topic of prayer itself only arise in chapter six?" The reviewer was objecting that, if the book was supposed to be about how to pray, why did I not talk about it until the very last chapter? This comment, like many comments in the reviews, was helpful in making me think and reflect on my whole approach. But after reflecting on it, I still feel that the order of material in the book is correct. I still feel that the real problem in praying is in the preliminaries, and that, unless these preliminaries are faced and the person properly disposed, techniques for meditating and so on won't really help.

Using terms that are familiar to those who know the spiritual exercises of St. Ignatius, I don't think you can come into the "second week" unless you've first passed through the "first week." The self-knowledge gained in the first week of the exercises is, I think, the purification experience which disposes us to be filled with Christ in the second week. I've noticed that in this day and age, when there's a strong stress on the resurrection in our spirituality, many of my students who study the four-week, thirty-day Ignatian exercises in my course on retreats don't like to spend much time on the first week. They want to get right into the mystery of Christ, which is treated more fully in the second week. I always have to stress to them that that's very dangerous, because the knowledge of self which comes in the first week of the exercises is the opening of ourselves that is necessary to be filled with Christ. It's like a flowerpot that's filled with dead, exhausted dirt. You can't simply replant and place new life in the flowerpot if you don't first empty out what's presently filling it. And so too, unless the first week—the emptying of the self— takes place, there can be no filling with the Lord.

In their concern today to get to the resurrection, therefore, people tend to bypass the necessary preliminary stages, the coming to quiet and to self-knowledge. Of course, we do in fact stress the need for quiet more today than we used to. Living in a pressurized age, many people are looking for tranquilizers, and often things like meditation are their tranquilizers. But the thing which is very much neglected is the self-knowledge, the honest self-confrontation without which we cannot encounter God.

THREE MEANS OF GAINING
SELF-KNOWLEDGE

I mentioned in *Opening to God* that the three main means to self-knowledge in our daily life that I can see, in addition to the first week of the Spiritual Exercises (which is probably the most valuable means I know), are the practice of penance, the examination of conscience (or consciousness), and the work of getting to know who God is.

Penance

I think maybe we can rediscover penance today in the liturgical season of Lent precisely because penance is much more optional and voluntary. After Vatican II, it seemed to some people that the deemphasizing of strict penitential requirements was a great loss. Today, for example, in the Philippines, we don't even have the mandatory abstinence on Fridays. The only two days which are mandatory fast and abstinence days are Ash Wednesday and Good Friday. All the other Fridays of the year, one is encouraged to either abstain or substitute some act of penance or charity.

The stress on penance since Pope Paul VI has been on flexibility, and not all find this to be a good thing. However, I think that as we grow we will realize that flexibility enhances the value of penance in our lives rather than diminishes it. It makes penance more a question of personal decision and personal choice. And that fits in very nicely with what I was trying to say about penance in *Opening to God*. Penance is a means to purification; it's not an end. God does not enjoy penance in and of itself. A religious congregation, I think, cannot be founded on penance. I know that some have been, but I think that's a mistake. Penance is not an end, and God does not enjoy it; it's merely a means. The real end must always be kept in view. But granted that, the means is necessary.

One of the very important things about penance is to let the punishment fit the crime, as Gilbert and Sullivan have taught us. Our penance, voluntarily chosen, should be suited to what we see is in need of purification in our lives. For example, somebody who eats like a bird would not be a very good candidate for fasting. That would not be a very helpful penance. I have had sisters on retreat who asked whether they should fast but admitted that they didn't particularly like to eat. Maybe a better penance for them would be to eat rather than to fast. I remember giving a retreat to a sister who was convinced by my talking that she should have more penance in her life, but she hated to eat, and so food was not a good penance for her. I said to her, "Well, how about reading?" I was just casting around because I didn't know her very well. She said, "Oh, I love to read." I said, "Well, maybe a good penance for you then would be to postpone reading the newspaper until after lunch each day." And she said, "Oh, that would be terrible!" She said, "I'm the first one in there in the morning to get the paper before anybody else." And I said, "Well, fine. There would be a good penance in the very area where your curiosity is very strong. You need to be informed"—she was a teaching sister— "you need to be informed, but you don't have to be informed before noontime. Nothing in your work will suffer if you wait until noontime to read the paper." So she told me that she thought that would be a very challenging penance! When I met with her a couple of years later—this was in Australia—I was delighted to have her say how helpful this penance had been, and how she had stuck to it. Why? Because it was a way of gaining control over her instinctual desires. In and of itself this is small.

There's no great intrinsic value in fasting—it is a training of the will. I would hope that my sister friend, because of that penance, learned to be more restrained in other, more important areas in her life, and that she would not spontaneously jump to every stimulus, even in more important and significant situations in her life, precisely because she had chosen to deliberately practice restraint in this relatively unimportant area.

Penance, then, is a very important part of purification. It's also an important way to self-knowledge. You can learn a lot about yourself by making resolutions and breaking them! You learn a lot about the quality of your will. You learn a lot about the kinds of things that are easy for you to do and the things that are difficult for you. If you mature, you learn a lot about your own selfishness and your own capacity for self-deception.

The Examen

Recognizing the reality of selfishness and of self-deception relates very much to the second type of purification, or, more accurately, the second instrument of purification, namely, the examen of conscience, or examination of conscience, or consciousness examined, as we call it today. Father George Ashenbrenner and others have written quite a bit, and beautifully so, about this whole idea of the consciousness examined, or the awareness examined, as some call it. I think it is a very, very important means to self-knowledge and purification. The image which has come to my mind since writing *Opening to*

God is that it is a form of exposure or *conscientization*. Here in the Philippines, we're very much concerned today with conscientization, with exposure in the area of social justice. In the United States as well, it is becoming more and more common to have students during their college years get exposed to the lives of the poor, the marginalized.

What are we doing when we invite students out from their university and expose them to the slum areas or the squatter areas? I don't think they are there primarily to help. When our seminarians go out for apostolate, I don't think the primary purpose is the work they are doing for the people because, if it was, it would not be very practical. Their studies and their formation take far too much of their time for such work to have much immediate effect. The amount of time they can give to the people is very limited, and it always has to take third priority to their prayer formation and their studies. If they are there primarily to help, this is not a very efficient way to do it. But I don't think that is why they are there. I think they are there to learn. They will spend the rest of their lives, once they are ordained, serving people and helping them. That will be their whole vocation.

The whole point of student ministry is more conscientization or exposure. When we send our college students from more affluent families out to the squatter areas, I don't think it's so much to change the squatter area today; rather, it's so that in the future, when the former students are business people and professional people, they won't pass a beggar on the street without seeing him. Because of their awareness exercise now, because of their exposure, their conscientization now, they will be sensitive to these things in their daily lives. And that's exactly the way I understand the examen, or examination of conscience. And it's the way I explain it to young people today. It hits home because it's very much rooted in their secular and social experience. The same way we expose people to poverty in order that they will see it in their daily lives, so too in the examen. We take time each day, usually in the evening, to let the whole day come before us in order to be exposed to what has been happening within us. Particularly when we're young, so many of the things that happen to us, we don't even notice. We don't see where God is working in the day. We don't see how we're responding. We're insensitive. The examen is a kind of sensitivity session where I come to quiet, and in that quiet I force myself to go back and look over the day at leisure and evaluate it, hopefully with God's light, to see where he has been speaking in the day, to see how I responded to the way he was speaking.

Of course, the purpose of the examen is not really to review the day. The purpose is so that tomorrow I will be more spontaneously sensitive when important things happen. That's why I think the examen is more important for beginners (although it's valuable all our lives). Later on as we grow, we should be more and more spontaneously sensitive. In a sense, mature, older pray-ers should be making the examen all the time, in the sense that they are alert to the situations of God speaking and the challenge of their responding as they happen. Experienced pray-ers don't have to wait until evening to recognize God speaking, but beginners do, because they don't yet have the sensitivity to see these things as they happen. In that sense, the examen is very important.

I feel that one of the shortcomings in *Opening to God* was that the above point about the examen was not developed quite fully enough. I would add to what I said in that book this one other point, which is very much dependent on Father Ashenbrenner and others who have written on the examen. The examen should be a review not only of my failures but of God's communications. It should be a review of how God has been speaking to me in the day's events. How has God been speaking through that person I clashed with? How has God been speaking through the poor, blind person I saw beside the street? How has God been speaking through my best friend with whom I was reunited today? How has God been speaking? Only after asking this question should I ask, "How have I responded?" Both dimensions must be present. The examen must be a review both of God's speaking and of my responding. When I review my failures, as we've been accustomed to calling them, they should be seen, not as failures measured against the law, but as failures to respond to the word God was speaking to me today. I always say to people, if our examen was like that, our review of the day would never be routine or boring. No two days would ever be alike because God is never speaking the same way in any two days. What we want to become sensitive to is not only our response, but *how* God speaks.

The Examen and the Sacrament

I would say the same thing about the Sacrament of Penance or Reconciliation, as we call it today. I will mention that I feel that the word reconciliation —this may be heretical today—this may not be such a good name for the sacrament. The reason is that I don't think we're always being reconciled to God. What I have in mind here is committed people, the kind of people who would read books such as this. For such people, there's unlikely to be very much malice in their lives. Therefore, there's not likely to be much need for reconciliation, at least not in the way that word is ordinarily understood in English.

The Sacrament of Reconciliation is about our relationship with God and sin, and I think we have to look at sin not just as malice, but as sickness. I think there are two kinds of sin in our lives. When there is malice, bad will, then we do in fact need to be reconciled—we need to be forgiven. But in the lives of committed people, that will be fairly rare. What is much more likely to be present in such a life is sin as sickness—the type of sin in Romans, chapter 7: "I see the good, and I want it, but I find myself doing something else." That type of sin will be very, very common in the lives of committed people, even holy people. St. James says the just man sins seven times a day. And that's the just man. So sin as weakness, sin as sickness, is going to be common in the lives even of committed people. But if we're sick, we don't need to be reconciled; we need to be healed. And this is why I think if we look at sin in two ways, we have to look at the Sacrament of Penance or Reconciliation in two ways also. If there's malice, I go there to be forgiven. But if there is sickness, I go there to be healed.

Now, if I'm correct in thinking this way about the sacrament—and I can't appeal to any great authorities here to support me—it answers a lot of questions that people ask. First of all, why should I go to confession over and over again when I keep committing the same sins? Well, obviously if there's malice, that's a correct criticism. That's a legitimate problem. If I have bad will and I confess week after week the same things, one can question one's sincerity. If I really have bad will this week, and then I say I'm sorry, and then I have bad will next week, something's very strange there, and you can begin to doubt your sincerity, as many people do. But if the sin I'm talking about is sickness, that is, I want the good and yet I seem unable to do it—in other words, the Romans 7 type of sin—in that case, it makes very good sense to keep going back. The analogy here would be the doctor. You go to your doctor—provided you trust your doctor—when you are sick, and you keep on going until you're healed. You don't stop because you went once and you weren't healed. You don't say to the doctor, "Well, I came last week and I was still sick this week, so what's the point of going again?" No, if you commit yourself to the doctor in trust, you're willing to keep coming back again and again until the healing takes place. So, too, the paralytic who was by the pool for thirty-eight years in St. John's Gospel—what if he had quit after thirty-seven years? Suppose he said in that thirty-seventh year, "This is too much. I keep coming, but nothing happens." Well, if he had said that, he would not have been there in the thirty-eighth year when the Lord came. And maybe he would never have been healed. He had to be humble enough to be willing to keep coming back until it was the Lord's time of healing. And it made good sense to keep coming back until he was healed.

To sum up, I would say that both the examination of conscience and the Sacrament of Reconciliation, to use the contemporary term, should focus in the same way on how God has been speaking and on how I have been responding. If my failures to respond are due to sickness, I have to be very patient with myself, very willing to keep coming back. I should not feel guilty in the sense of committing sins of bad will, but I should be very humbled by my inability to do the good that I want, and, therefore, more and more dependent upon the Lord to make possible in me what is clearly impossible by my own efforts alone. This, I think, unites the examen and the sacrament. And I always suggest to people with regard to the sacrament that, where there is not sin of malice but of sickness, one would do well to confess in the same way one goes through the examen. That is, to first of all confess where they have most encountered God since their last confession.

For example, one might confess, "My last confession was three weeks ago, and in that time I have been most aware of God's presence in some of my friends who have supported me when I was feeling low, particularly one very difficult time. In light of that, I feel that I have failed to respond to God's love by not being sensitive enough to the suffering of others, not being supportive enough when others were low, period." I think that's a very good confession. I do not think that one needs to give a catalog of all the ways in which he or she needs to be healed. If it helps to use what I would call the "laundry-list" approach to confession, that is, to enumerate all the laundry in detail, fine. But I think many people today do not find that too helpful, and to them I would say I don't think it's really necessary.

For example, suppose you go to the doctor with acute appendicitis, and he rushes you to the operating table and starts to cut you open, and before he knocks you out, you say, "Oh, by the way, doctor, I also have an ingrown toenail, so I'd be glad if you take care of that while you're removing my appendix." Well, that's a little silly. Sure, the doctor could take care of the toenail, but maybe it's more important to save your life first. You don't have to do everything at once. So I think it's good to acknowledge the main failure—that for which I'm specifically coming for healing, and then I can say, "I ask the Lord's healing for everything else, but I would like to focus this sacrament particularly here, where I feel the need to respond to him." I think that is a much sounder practice, psychologically and spiritually.

Getting to Know the Lord: The Imagination

Having gone over techniques of coming to quiet and techniques of purification, the final techniques I would like to talk about are techniques of meditation using, in the Ignatian sense, the imagination. These too are techniques not of praying per se, but are techniques of getting to know something *of* God. It's like the difference between reading up on some distinguished figure that I'm planning to meet, and then actually meeting him or her. No matter how much I read, I won't really know the person in the same way as I will when I meet him or her. What I'm saying is, there are techniques of reading up on people. There are no techniques of meeting them. And when that person is God, it is even more so, because God is the Lord of the encounter.

To help make clear what I mean by learning something *of* God, I will extend my radio analogy from earlier. We said earlier that in order to play the radio, you need both quiet and a well-tuned and well-functioning machine, and that's what our whole purification discussion was about—tuning the radio in and making sure that the batteries are in working order. Our "radio," in other words, needs to be functioning well to receive God. When I wrote *Opening to God*, I remember at the time being puzzled about how the last chapter would fit into that radio analogy, and in the end I did not fit it in. But it has occurred to me since then that one more thing is necessary.

I enjoy listening to classical music on my radio. Now, in order to really enjoy classical music, in addition to quiet and a well-working, well-tuned radio, I will likely need, as a matter of preparation, a good course in music appreciation. I think that this need to train one's mind and ear so as to appreciate the music extends and completes our analogy perfectly. The meditative stage of our prayer lives is like a good course in music appreciation. No matter how quiet you are, and no matter how well your radio is working, you won't appreciate classical music (most people won't) unless they have some sort of instruction in what it's all about. Classical music is an acquired taste. Normally people have to grow into it.

I remember once giving a retreat, and at this retreat one of my favorite teaching devices was spoiled. One of my favorite retreat devices was to play Handel's *Messiah* at table. Once, in a place and with a congregation that will remain nameless here, after the lunch, while the soprano had been singing "I know that my redeemer lives," one of the old sisters came up to me and said, "Do you realize she repeated the same thing thirty-eight times?" Well, this ruined the music for me! I was playing it in order to help their prayer, and she was sitting there counting the number of times a phrase was sung! To her, it was just boring repetition. She didn't get anything out of the *Messiah*.

I suppose if I were ever to try to share with the sister what I got out of the *Messiah*, I would have to explain to her why Handel has the soloists repeat. What's the point of the repetition? Was it just that he couldn't think of anything else to say, or that the record got stuck? Or is there real artistic purpose to the repetition? The sister would likely never discover the purpose for herself, unless somebody sat down and told her, "This is the way an oratorio is constructed. This is precisely what the composer is trying to do with the human voice as an instrument." And this is precisely how we grow in understanding. You see, her problem about repeating the phrase in the *Messiah* indicates that she would have been somewhat hard up with most of our prayer lives, where we do a lot of repetition of familiar phrases and familiar prayers. Why do we repeat? Because the repetition makes the meaning go deeper.

So, in addition to quiet and purification, we're going to need to get to know the Lord in our prayer. And that "getting to know" is going to involve a sort of course in "music appreciation," that is, an appreciation of who God is. That's precisely what we go to the scripture for. Simply reading scripture is not praying in its essential sense, any more than a course in music appreciation is really enjoying good music. It's too mechanical for that. Someone who has really learned to love good music would find a course in music appreciation rather boring, even frustrating. They want to listen to the music. They don't want somebody talking or offering explanations, they want experience. So, too, pray-ers will eventually find that the "getting to know" phase of their prayer life also passes away.

But in the beginning, we need to explore the scriptures, because that's where we get to know the Lord, precisely in order to find out what Jesus' values are, what kind of person he is, what it's going to mean to be his friend. We can't really love him unless we're attuned to him, just as in my analogy someone cannot love good music unless they have the taste for it. Another way of putting it is that, in the first stage of our prayer, we're acquiring a taste for God as God really is.

PART TWO:

FROM KNOWING TO
LOVING

I n discussing the life of prayer, one of the things I have stressed very much in books, talks, and in my formation work with seminarians is that prayer is *growth*, prayer is *life*. Now, anything that is living must either be changing in the sense of growth or it must be dying. Living things are always changing. That's why we cannot stand still, any more than an animal or even a fower can just stand still. We're always moving, either growing or regressing.

Prayer life, since it's life, is also characterized by that dynamic quality. It cannot stand still. It has to be either growing and changing or dying. That is the basic perspective on prayer I put forward in both *Opening to God* and *When the Well Runs Dry*. Prayer has the dynamic perspective of something that is changing. What is appropriate to us at one point in our prayer lives is not appropriate at another. That's basically the point which I would like to discuss in this second part, the dynamics of growth in prayer, in which we move from getting to know God to loving God.

HE, THOU, AND
YOU

We have already discussed some of the prerequisites for prayer. We ended part 1 with the idea that it was essential in prayer to begin to get to know God. In this second part, I would like to offer the idea that we can see patterns of growth in our prayer if we look carefully at the ways in which we name God.

For example, to call God "he" would, among other things, imply that somehow God is around the corner or in the next room. To call God "he" implies that God is someone whose existence I believe in but is someone with whom I don't have direct personal experience. You might talk about my mother as "she" since you've never met her. She would not be "thou" or "you" or "beloved" to you because you've never encountered her.

I think that the God of most people is probably "he." That is, most people haven't met God personally, at least they don't know that they have. For that reason, while many people "believe" in God, God doesn't really play much of a part in their lives. Therefore, God remains "he."

However, when God becomes "thou," the relationship becomes personal. I say "thou" to someone with whom I am face-to-face. Of course, "thou" is scarcely used in English. English speakers don't have much way of differentiating between the reverential "thou" and the more familiar "you," but many languages do. For example, here in Tagalog we distinguish between *kayo* or *ikaw*. Spanish does the same, as does German. There are many ways in many languages of differentiating between the reverential and the familiar personal address. English can do it by means of "thou," but "thou" is somewhat antiquated; it's not a word one normally uses. It only comes up in old prayers and things like that, maybe because our American culture is so democratic and egalitarian. "Thou" doesn't really have the place that it would have in most cultures. However, it still helps form a useful illustration. If God is "thou," then the relationship is personal, but it is one of master to servant. If God is "you," the relationship is one of equality, of people standing face-to-face as friends. And strangely enough, many people, even people with the beginnings of a real relationship to God, prefer the "thou."

Why should this be? Why would people prefer "thou"? For one thing, "thou" indicates the Old Testament relationship of master and servant. This means that the relationship is marked by mutual responsibilities and obligations that are clearly defined. A servant knows when he has finished his duties. He knows when he's free. If I work from nine to five, when it's five o'clock, I have no obligation to the owner. I'm perfectly free to go home and forget about the employer and think of my family. I have no obligation to be alert to the employer. If the employer calls me in the middle of the night, I am in no way obligated to get out of bed in order to accommodate him.

The advantage of the servant/master relationship is that the responsibilities and the obligations are both clearly defined and limited. Most of us prefer that because, if God were our friend and equal, there would be no time off. We are never "finished" with friends. A friend can never say, "I have done everything I need to do, and therefore I can relax and think only of myself." Real friendship doesn't allow for that. When Jesus says in the Last Supper discourse in St. John's Gospel, "I call you no longer servants but friends," I think what he's doing there is contrasting the two covenants, the old covenant relationship of servant and master, and the new covenant relationship of friend.

Oftentimes, when I give retreats to sisters, I will say to them, "I'd like you to think over today on this point, how many of you are really Old Testament people?" I suspect the answer is most of us are Old Testament people. We prefer the relationship of servant to master, although we would say, "Oh no, I don't," but I think really we do. I think this because so often we live our lives that way. We want to know our responsibilities, we want to know when we're finished. We don't want God demanding too much of our lives and therefore we like the situation of the servant. When Jesus says, "I call you no longer servants but friends," I think that in their hearts most people would say, "No thanks; I'd rather be a servant. I'd rather remain in the Old Testament. I'd rather not get entangled in the demands of friendship."

To make the point concrete, let me recall an incident that was very significant in my life. My father died in 1973, and I had the experience of being home with him during the last three weeks of his life. One of the people whom I met at that time was Mrs. Kim, a Korean woman who was a nurse in the hospital where my father was. Of all the nurses taking care of my father, she was the best. My father trusted her totally, and all of us thought she was a very good nurse.

On the Saturday evening before my father died (he died on a Thursday), Mrs. Kim came into the hospital room when my family members were there, and she said to my father, "Mr. Green, I'm leaving tonight for my vacation, and I'll be back in two weeks. I'll be away for two weeks, so I will see you when I get back. Now you take care." Now, we knew and my father knew (and Mrs. Kim knew) that most likely my father would be dead before she came back. But no one could complain about her words, or about her taking vacation. This was quite legitimate. If Mrs. Kim had to wait for all of her patients to be out of danger or to die before she left, she would never get vacation. It was too bad that it was my father that was dying at the time, but none of us could complain about that. She had to go on vacation. Her relationship was that of a servant at its best—I don't mean to use that word in a bad sense. What I mean is she had responsibilities to my father that were contractual. She had deeper responsibilities elsewhere. The servant relationship can of course be very loving, as it was with her, but, still, the obligations are limited. They're not open-ended. And Mrs. Kim never saw my father again.

Now suppose that, instead of my father's nurse, my mother came into the hospital room that same Saturday evening and said to my father, "George, I'm leaving for my vacation tonight. I hope you're still alive when I get back." Now, that would be indecent! No wife who loved her husband could ever do that. That's precisely the contrast between a servant and a friend. What was legitimate for Mrs. Kim would be obscene for my mother—it would be unimaginable.

Perhaps this story can make clear why many people prefer to remain servants in their relationship to God. The reason is that being friends is costly. When you are a friend, you cannot say, "I have my fulfilled my responsibility." I think that's why Jesus says in another part of the scripture, "When you have done all that you are *supposed* to do, simply say, 'We are unprofitable servants. We have only done what we were supposed to do.'" This passage puzzled me for years. But I think what Jesus means is that, when we have fulfilled our formal obligations, we have only done what the servant does, namely, what he or she should do. Until we get beyond the "should" to some kind of unconditional surrender of the whole self, which is much more than the "should," we cannot even begin to talk of friendship; we are merely servants. I think that in that passage Jesus is likely contrasting the two states.

To name God "thou," then, captures a more formal personal relationship, but the theme of friendship (as opposed to servanthood) is better expressed as "you," at least as I understand it in this little scheme that I've described. I think naming someone as "you" or "beloved" means friendship that has reached fruition, has reached maturity, and has reached a level of total self-giving, which is promised in the "you" of the friend. It takes a long time growing together and living together to realize this.

In terms of prayer life, I would like to suggest that these words describe a progression that can indicate for us various stages of growth in our interior life.

THREE STAGES OF
GROWTH

I see three stages of growth in the life of prayer, stages which I have described in my other books as "getting to know," "from knowing to loving," and "from loving to truly loving." Getting to know is the topic of *Opening to God*; from knowing to loving is the theme of first part of *When the Well Runs Dry*; from loving to truly loving is the theme of the second part of *Well*. What I would I'd like to suggest here is a slightly different way of looking at those themes, a fresh way of looking at them. I would also like to suggest that these three stages are a way of bringing one's relationship with God from the "he" to the "beloved," via the "thou" and then the "you." It's precisely the interpersonal relationship to God, the personal encounter with God, which will be very different at the "thou" level and the "you" level and the "beloved" level. Deepening personal encounter is precisely what is accomplished by means of these stages.

We can distinguish these three stages of growth from one another by asking ourselves, what is it that we go to prayer for? I think that, in the first stage, the getting to know, we go to prayer in order to gain insight, in order to gain understanding. That meditative, imaginative phase of our prayer is ordered toward knowledge of God so that we may come to love him; but we cannot love what we do not first know. In order for me to be able to love God, it's necessary first to know God, and therefore the purpose of that first stage of prayer exists to gain insight into who God is and who I am by contrast. What kind of person is God? What are God's values? What does God demand of others? What does God give to others? The focus of stage one is on understanding and insight. Before I commit myself to this relationship, I want to know who it is that I am committing to.

In prayer, just as with any young man and woman who are courting, a hasty marriage is very dangerous—you can easily find yourself waking up married to a stranger. It's necessary to have time to get to know who this person I'm attracted to really is. What are their values? I don't want to base the marriage just on emotion, because that will never last. It never has lasted, and it never will. So, who really is this person, and for that matter who am I, and how do we mesh? What do I find in this person which I desire for myself? What's it going to cost me? Where will I have to change to live lovingly with this person? All of that has to be explored in the first stage. The focus of the first stage is on insight and understanding. It's on getting to know God.

In the second stage, (the main subject of this chapter) the focus is more on experiencing God. In the second stage, we fall in love. We focus here not so much on knowing who God is but on experiencing God, on being with God in love and sharing our lives. In this stage, there is a great focus on experience. This is when people will be very concerned with whether or not they can feel God's presence in their prayer, and are very disturbed when they cannot feel the presence, when God seems to be absent. Notice, by the way, that for somebody who's still in the first stage, it doesn't make much sense to talk about the absence of God. People who are still at the beginning don't really feel God's absence because they haven't really known the presence. Someone cannot be absent to me unless that person has formerly been present, and therefore, as I will talk more about later, absence is, paradoxically, really a form of presence. That will be a very important insight as we progress.

The third stage in prayer life is the stage of "from loving to truly loving." In this third stage, we go to prayer not for insight, nor for an experience. Rather, we go to give God joy. In terms of ourselves, we go to be transformed. If we talk about the third stage in terms of what we seek for ourselves, what we're seeking is not to understand God or even to experience God—it's to be transformed by God. We'll have to explain more about how that has to happen later, but, basically, we need to become transformed because the real, ultimate goal of prayer life is to become divine. The friendship of the you and, ultimately, the beloved is only possible between equals. God can only be beloved to me when I have become divine. That's why it's dangerous to try to jump ahead too much, to be too familiar beyond the actual point of our relationship. Even with us human beings, that's true. I personally find it somewhat offensive, or pushy, when people want to be too familiar with me when I don't yet know them very well. You feel there's a certain near-indecency about it when they become your nickname buddies and you just met them today. They're jumping too fast into familiarity and intimacy, and normally that will frighten people away. It has the opposite of its intended effect. If somebody tries to take possession of me too fast, I'm likely to stand back and try to avoid them. You don't want to be possessed until you freely give yourself.

The same thing is true with God. In order to be beloved of him, and for God to be beloved of us, we have to reach a certain level of equality. We have to be divinized, as the scriptures say. The First Letter of John says in chapter 3, verse 2, "We do not know what we will be. We know what we are now, children of God. But this much we know about the future: that we will be like him. That we will know him as he is." This, in a way, points to the idea of divinization, and there are other passages in scripture which may not be as explicit, especially in St. John and St. Paul, which point in the same direction. It makes sense, because friendship can only be between equals.

I have a friend here, a lady who's a widow and has grown children, and she has a girl working for her as a kind of a servant. But since my friend is a very good-hearted person, and since this girl who works for her has been with her many years, the girl has become almost like a sister and a member of the family. But that sometimes creates problems in the relationship, because my friend gets very frustrated when she tries to give her maid orders. The maid talks back. The reason the maid talks back is because my friend has, to an extent, made her a friend. My friend has a difficulty—she's not sure whether she wants the maid to be a maid or a friend. The difficulty lies in that you can't have both. If I treat somebody like a sister, I can't order the person around. If I order a person around, I can't treat her like a sister. If I try to be both simply because I want to be democratic, I somehow lose my authority. That's what has happened to my friend. Now, I think that deep down, she's happy to have lost her authority. She complains about it jokingly. She says, "I'm paying her, and then she tells me what to do." Sure, well that's because she's made her a member of the family. The same thing, I think, happens with God. If we are to truly live in love with him, we have to become like him, we have to become members of the family, and that's a very gradual process of growth.

So, in the third stage of a good prayer life, after the knowing and the experiencing (which may initially seem like knowing the beloved, but it's really not—it's really much earlier in the relationship at that point), begins the crucial work of divinization, or transformation. The earlier experience of God in our prayer lives is more like the transfiguration experience. It's a sign of coming attractions. It's a promise of what will be in the future, but it's not fully real yet. Peter thought when the transfiguration took place that they could just stay there forever, but he was wrong. They had a lot of suffering and dying to do first. What God was showing them was what would be at the end if they were faithful. But they weren't ready for it yet, contrary to what Peter thought.

So too with us, that initial consolation, that initial emotional experience of God in prayer in the early years looks and feels like we have achieved real intimacy and real holiness. It's really more of a coming attraction, I think, like the transfiguration. And after the Lord has gotten us hooked on himself, then he says, "Okay, now we have to go about the serious business of transformation. You're going to have to let me work to make you divine if you're ever going to realize the kind of union with me that you desire." That will be the third phase in a good prayer life. So, we go to God to know God, we go for insight, for experience, and then for transformation. And I think the whole thrust of that process is precisely to lead us from the "he" to the "beloved."

BETWEEN TALKING AND
LISTENING

L et's look a bit more at the basic pattern of transformation. If we were to put it in a very simple,
very down-to-earth fashion, it's the move from talking to listening. I mentioned earlier the experience of
my Protestant minister friends who have found that
in their own traditions prayer is mostly talking, petition. When they read my books, they began to feel
like they had found something that was lacking in
their lives and which they were seeking. I also mentioned that in my own experience with prayer
groups, and with sisters and priests and brothers and
laypeople who come to me for direction, the same
thing is generally true of Catholics as well. Catholics

also tend to think of praying as talking, and don't always know how to listen. They don't even know what it would mean for God to talk. And since we're all afraid, embarrassed, and uncomfortable with waiting for results, we end up talking all the time.

Did you ever notice that when you're with someone you don't know very well and don't yet feel secure with, you keep talking all the time? Your mouth runs off and you don't know why. We often say very foolish things with strangers we're not comfortable with, simply because we're even more uncomfortable listening to them. We're afraid of the silence, whereas with people we know very well, people we love, we're quite comfortable with silence. You don't have to be talking all the time. When I'm directing seminarians or other people who are new to the interior life and spiritual direction, they're very uncomfortable if we don't talk for thirty seconds. With people I've grown to know and have worked with for some time, I can sit in silence and be very comfortable while the person is digesting what has been said, while they're thinking of what might come next.

Now, since we don't see God in the way we see other people, the unease and the embarrassment can be twice as bad. We are unsure of the new person we can see. But we are even more unsure of somebody when we're not even sure if there's anybody there—somebody we cannot see with our bodily eyes. So we end up in our prayer being very talkative and being very poor listeners. Not only that, we find that we're afraid of silence.

So what I would like to develop next is the idea that the affective prayer, the experiential prayer (the second stage), is a bridge between talking and listening. I'd like to explore how God uses that experience of consolation in the middle of our prayer lives to lead us from being very talkative to being good listeners.

To give a very simple schematization of that whole threefold pattern of growth that I described earlier and the place the second stage has in it, it might be worth answering a question that is brought up often by my directees and retreatants: can one go back and forth, between the insightful, the experiential, and the transformative, between the focus on thinking, the focus on feeling, and the focus on transforming? I think a person can, although I wouldn't describe it so much as going "back and forth" between stages. Rather, what I would say is that, at any given point in our lives, one mood or one type of experience predominates but not to the exclusion of the others.

For example, even in the early years of one's prayer life, the very early years, although the primary focus will be on knowledge, we will experience some affection. We would not persevere if there were absolutely none. When our prayer becomes more experiential and more affective, there will still be some insight gained, although this will be less central than in that initial stage. Even in the stage of the dry well, which we'll talk about later, there will be some times of affective prayer and there will be some times of insight. These moments will be experienced like oases in the desert then, but they will still happen. So, I would define these stages as not clear-cut, sharply-distinguished phases, but as stages that gradually shade one into the other. The gaining of insight gradually, very gradually, shifts into a more affective approach, so that for some time the two will be mixed together. Even when the affective begins to predominate, there will still be times of insight. So with that as a background, it's an important point to note that we are not looking to sharply delimit these stages. In fact, I'd like to again suggest that the affective stage provides a kind of bridge between talking to God and listening to God.

When I speak about affective prayer, what I mean is when our prayer is more devotional, when the feelings are strong, when there's a great deal of loving God, when a little scripture goes a long way. In the very beginning of my prayer life, I might have needed to read pages and pages of scripture to get anything out of it; now I may read just a few verses and that's sufficient for the whole hour. A small amount sustains me. My feelings and the peace in my soul are quite sufficiently fed by just a little bit, and I go to scripture not so much to discover as to remember.

When my father died, my family crafted death cards specially for him. We spoke of him and remembered him with joy. When I go home every few years, my brother and sister and I love to get my mother to talk about him and tell about the good old days: what happened when they were courting, what happened when we were kids, what happened when we were in school, what happened when they used to go away to the insurance conventions. Most of what she tells us today we know already. We get very little new information. Occasionally she says something which surprises me, but most of the time it's a matter of singing the old songs again.

Why do we like my mother to tell us things we already know? "Tell us about the time that Dad drove out to California through the Grand Canyon. Tell us about when you were sitting in the back of the car." My sister and she were sitting in the back of the car with their feet in a bucket of ice because the desert temperature was about 115 degrees. Now, there's no new information there. We've heard it many times before. Why do we like to hear it again? Not for information, but for remembering. And because remembering someone we love moves the heart. That's the kind of affective prayer I'm speaking about here, where even our reflection is not so much used for new knowledge, but to move the heart. And when we go to scripture, that's what we go for, to read about somebody we love in order that our love may be stirred.

GOD BECOMES REAL:

PREPARING FOR

CONTEMPLATION

B uilding on what I mean by affective prayer, I would like to pick up an idea from Fr. William Conley, a Jesuit who has written a very fine article in the series "Studies in the Spirituality of Jesuits." His article is on spiritual direction, theology, and practice in which he points out that the goal of direction is contemplation. The purpose of spiritual direction—and this is the way I understand spiritual direction also—is to facilitate contemplation, and therefore the role of a good director is not to be a problem solver, although he may do some of that; it's not to give advice, although he may also do some of that. The role of the director is primarily and centrally to facilitate contemplation.

Now what Fr. Conley means by contemplation is not floating up to the ceiling, having visions, hearing mystical voices, or smelling roses when there are no roses around. As St. John of the Cross insists, true contemplation has nothing to do with preternatural phenomena. Rather, what Fr. Conley means by contemplation is that moment when Jesus becomes personally real to me, when God becomes personally real to me. Fr. Conley says that spiritual direction actually divides into two phases, pre- and post-contemplation. And the role of a director prior to contemplation, prior to the moment when God becomes personally real to the directee, is to be like John the Baptist, pointing out the Lord, trying to suggest where the directee, who has not yet met Jesus, might meet him. "Try this. Do that. Let me know what happens." The director encourages ways of facilitating the encounter.

Once contemplation takes place, that is, once God becomes personally real to the directee, the director's role becomes very different. The director becomes, at this point, not a guide to experience, but rather an interpreter of that experience. An interpreter is needed because there are other counterfeit voices around. There are people and there are devils trying to sound like God, trying to imitate Jesus

Christ. There are other gospels being preached besides the authentic gospel, and even the good can be deceived, as St. Paul stresses very often. We can be deceived by these other voices and these other gospels and false messiahs who appear in the guise of Jesus and can even lead astray the saints. For that reason, for those who have experienced contemplation, the director becomes an interpreter of the experience, not so much a mediator of it. And for that reason, direction is going to be very different pre- and post- contemplation.

What I want to emphasize in Fr. Conley's scheme—because his article really is excellent as a guide to direction—is the idea of the experience of Jesus as the moment of contemplation, that is, that moment when God becomes personally real to me. That's what *I* mean by affective prayer. Sometimes people who are very romantic create a fantasy God of their own, and they can have a lot of affection for a god they have not encountered, but created. Loving a god created in one's own image is the problem of infatuation. Teenagers are normally infatuated with several people. They fall in love with their fellow students. They fall in love with their teachers. They fall in love with celebrities. They fall in love with almost anybody available at one time or another. But they don't really love the person they are "in love" with. They love their romantic ideal of the person. I'm not talking about this kind of love. Real love, whether it be for a fellow human being or for God, is, in fact, more *realistic*. Once the hard work of getting to know God has taken place and we have our feet on the ground, the heart gets involved, and this God whom I know something about in turn reveals himself to me. When that God captures my heart, then you're talking about God having become personally real to me.

Now, interestingly enough, when that happens, when God becomes personally real to me, prayer inevitably becomes more receptive and less active in a way. Someone else (in this case, God) has become real and active to me, with me, in my life. As long as I'm the one writing the script, as long as I'm creating the play, I don't have to be dependent on anybody else; I control everything. I control the beginning, I control the ending, I control the characters, and I can be totally active and manipulative. However, once someone else becomes personally real to me, inevitably I become more receptive, because I never know what mood my friend will be in.

If my friend is a fantasy friend, I don't have to worry about how they will feel tomorrow. If you get up in the morning and you have a friend who's the product of your own imagination, you don't normally say, if you're in good mental health, "I wonder how my imaginary friend will be feeling today." You don't have to worry about that because you created him; he can be feeling however you want. But once you encounter a real, live friend, a flesh-and-blood friend, you can't be sure how they will be feeling today. You can't be sure how they will be talking to you. It's out of your control. And for that reason, once God becomes personally real to us, we inevitably become more receptive, less in control. Therefore, I think that as we grow in prayer, God gradually moves us through the experience of "from talking to listening."

However, in affective prayer we are still quite active. It's a sort of middle ground—or bridge—between the receptivity or passivity of encountering someone else, and the activity which normally accompanies emotional prayer, where there's a great stress on resolutions, affections, and on seeking to create the climate of experience so that we can reproduce the encounter at will.

LEARNING TO
GIVE

As human beings grow in relationship and become more dependent on one another, in many ways they are still quite manipulative. This is, in part, because our feelings and our emotions are essentially appetites. That means that they never give; they only take. Nobody has a generous stomach or a generous set of lungs. Our organs and our appetites are all taking. That's what it means to be an appetite. They don't give. There's never been a generous stomach yet. When the stomach starts giving out, that's unfortunate. What it's supposed to do is take in, and that's precisely what it's for. Our emotions as appetites are the same way. They are not by definition generous; they're self-seeking.

When we begin to experience God in our emotions, we inevitably try to control the encounter. We try to find ways to produce God at will. And this is because our emotions are appetites. We try, even in our generous moments, to take control of the situation, to make resolutions about how we are going to conquer the world for Christ: what I'm going to do for him. And what we're doing for him is not really as altruistic, that is, as other-centered, as we might think because we find ourselves daydreaming about the motto for our canonization, and we find ourselves thinking of what the church and the congregation will think of us after we've died, when they realize what a treasure they have had in their midst and how little they appreciated it at the time. This is the point that we have to see regarding feelings: our feelings can often be manipulative, and in the urge to feed them we're nearly always seeking to take over. And this happens at the very time that God, by encountering us as someone real, is taking the control out of our hands.

For example, when people marry, I suspect that very often they marry a project. This is a very dangerous thing to do. I think many people who marry, as they are walking down that aisle, have great plans regarding what they are going to make out of this other person, what he or she is going to be like in twenty-five years, after I get finished refashioning the person according to my image. I always tell people that this is a real and very dangerous temptation. I always say to people who talk to me about whether they will marry a certain person, "If you can't love the person who's right there, now, don't marry him (or her). Don't marry your ideal for the future because that person may never exist. If you can't love the person as he or she is, with all of his or her faults, don't. It's very dangerous to marry with a view to what you are going to make of your spouse because you're most likely to be deeply frustrated."

I think the same thing happens in our relations to God. We tend to want to control our relationships, but we can control God no more than we can control a person—less, in fact. It's far less likely that we would be able to control God, considering who God is, than a spouse would be able to control his or her partner in a relationship.

What gradually happens at this stage is that the Lord dries up our attempts to control and manipulate, so that even in the stage of affective prayer, our attempts to control the situation, our attempts to produce the feelings that we want, our attempts to manipulate the emotions, they gradually, if we're lucky, become more and more frustrated. We tend not to see it as lucky at the time, but what the Lord is trying to do, even in this stage of affective prayer, is to teach us to let God be the boss. And this is why you find that intermittent dryness in prayer, where even in the stage of affective prayer, when there's a good bit of feeling and experience involved, the Lord gradually seems to come and go unpredictably. One day God is very close; the next day God seems far away. Mondays, Wednesdays, and Fridays I'm flying high; Tuesdays, Thursdays, and Saturdays, it seems like God doesn't exist. That gradual drying up of our ability to control things is precisely the Lord's way of beginning to purify our affections by asserting that we are not in control.

What is the effect of that change, that move to the affections and the gradual purifying of them which begins in this stage, where we move to the heart and then lose control of the heart? What would be the effect of this on the initial progress we have made? What would be the effect on our coming to quiet? We spoke earlier of quieting ourselves down, learning techniques like yoga and Zen and mantras and using nature's scenery and scriptural passages—all the various ways we can come to quiet. In this next stage, in which our prayer has become more affective, there's not so much need for that kind of coming to quiet. What is meant by coming to quiet here, I think, is rather a letting go of ideas and structures of prayer, of formal structures which we learned in the novitiate—these are the things that make us unquiet at the second stage of maturity.

Many people never realize this, and they end up spending their whole lives struggling to pray as they prayed when they were novices. They end up frustrating what God is doing in their very efforts to maintain the structures they are familiar with. The great liberating experience of their life is when they realize that to come to quiet in this second stage of affective prayer is precisely to let go of all techniques and all structures and all ideas which in any way interfere with the Lord's free coming and going. "I must, because I was taught to do so, make the three preludes and the three points and the collect—even if God carries me away in ecstasy as I try—I have to go through the three points as I go flying through the heavens!" That's foolish. "I have to recite my rosary as the Lord carries me off." That's silly. But it's a kind of silliness which is very common in my experience as a director. So many people never grow because they're too busy fulfilling their obligations, and it's precisely here that we have to have the sensitivity to recognize the difference between these things which are means for getting to know and meet God and what is needed once we already know God, once we have already met him.

In other words, once we begin to know God, the relationship itself has to dictate what is proper. We can't dictate it by precooked and preconceived structures. In any relationship, there has to be flexibility. If I fall in love with somebody, before I decide what to do next, I have to look and see how that person is feeling and doing. To take a rather silly example, suppose somebody tells me, "In order to have a good marriage, you must always begin the day smiling, and when you first wake up you should say something cheerful and light-hearted to your spouse." So I resolve to practice that, and it works well.

As we get adjusted to one another in the marriage, this seems like a very nice practice. But then I feel, because I'm too inflexible, I must do this all the rest of my life. When I get up in the morning and my wife is deathly ill and she is vomiting in the bathroom, the first thing I have to do is tell her a joke because this is the way I learned to start every day. If I get up in the morning and she's grieving over the death of our eldest son, the first thing that I have to do is tell her a joke because this is what I was taught when I made the Pre-Cana Conference. That kind of rigidity will destroy love, and that's precisely the point I am making. At this point, the coming to quiet means the freedom to let the situation dictate the proper response, not to be a slave of structures and techniques and expectations of what should be happening.

Sometimes we are doubtful about whether we really should let go of structures. Many times we're not sure. Should I just wait and let the Lord take over in my prayer, or should I be more dependent on what I have learned? Maybe if I let go of structure, I'll be just drifting and going nowhere. If I let go of the patterns of prayer that I learned as a beginner, I may be presumptuous and lazy and I may drift aimlessly. On the other hand, if I cling to these patterns, I may interfere with God's taking over.

✓ I have found it very helpful to tell people that when this happens, tell the Lord in the first fifteen minutes of your prayer that you're doubtful about whether you should let go of the structures or not. When you come to pray, after preparing, say to the Lord, "Ok, Lord, the first fifteen or twenty minutes, I will just wait. I will give this time to you. If you want to take over, fine. I'll give you a chance to take over first. So during the first fifteen minutes, if it's distracted, okay. That's your problem. If it's blank, okay. If it's ecstatic, wonderful. But the point is, I have no control; these first ten or fifteen minutes I give to you to do whatever you want." And then, if after that time you find yourself very restless and it seems useless, then you can get to work reflecting, using your techniques, following your accustomed practices, and you don't have to worry that you're interfering with God. You gave God a chance to take over.

At the same time, you don't have to worry whether you're just being lazy because, after the first fifteen minutes, you can get to work if God doesn't seem to take the initiative. I have found this a very good way for people to act when they are doubtful about whether or not they should be more passive. I think it might be helpful for all of us, keeping in mind the realization that what we want to do eventually is to let go of anything that interferes with or in any way restricts the Lord's control over what is happening.

PART THREE:

FROM LOVING TO TRULY
LOVING

I n the first two parts, we discussed the basic ideas of prayer as opening, as encounter, as growth, and as relationship. I wrote that one of the basic ways of describing what God is doing in us is bringing us from prayer as talking to prayer as listening; prayer as something we do to prayer as something that is done to us. And I mentioned that there are three basic stages of prayer: the first stage, the "getting to know," where we are quite active and inquiring and exploring. God is of course the one teaching us—but in our searching of the scriptures and our questioning of life and our seeking of understanding of who God is, we're quite active.

The second stage is where prayer moves from the head to the heart, where prayer becomes more affective. I suggested that we could see this more affective prayer stage as a bridge between "prayer as activity" and "prayer as receptivity"; it can be seen as a bridge between prayer as talking and prayer as listening. The core of this affective prayer, the "from knowing to loving" phase, is precisely the experience of God or of Jesus as personally real to us, not just as somebody that we create out of our own fantasy, or somebody that we ourselves romanticize, but as someone we encounter in reality.

I have had many retreatants ask questions about differences between authentic affective prayer and fantasy prayer. One of the best criteria I know for determining the real experience of God is that, as St. John of the Cross said when someone asked him whether we know it's really God we're encountering and not just ourselves: "The best proof that it's God and not just ourselves is the fact that he is absent when we want him and present when we don't want him," or perhaps more accurately, present when we don't expect him. In other words, if we are writing the script, if we're fantasizing, we can make things happen when we want them to happen. We can create our own "experience" of God. We can turn God on and off at will, like the water faucet. Maybe not entirely at will because sometimes we may not be feeling well, or we may be tired and our imagination may not be working as well as usual, but there will be a basic pattern of controllability. Whereas the best proof that it's really God and not just my own imagination is that I cannot do that. In authentic prayer, God resists manipulation and doesn't come exactly when I want, no matter what techniques or tricks I use. If the prayer is authentic, God comes when I don't expect it, and sometimes when I would prefer that God not come, so that I find myself not controlling the situation.

In affective prayer, where we begin to experience God as real, there is a growing receptivity, because God takes more control of the relationship—it's not subject to our manipulation. Yet at the same time, we are quite active, and we do keep trying to manipulate our affections and resolutions. We find a beautiful place to pray, and then we try to recapture the same place at the same time. If we have experienced God at sunset while sitting under a tree in the lotus posture, we find ourselves going back to the same tree at the same time of day and crossing our legs in the same way.

We try to find some magic formula for reproducing spiritual experience. If we are lucky, God will resist this attempt. We will find that what worked

CONTEMPLATION: PURIFYING
TRANSFORMATION

I t is now time to say something about that third stage, which is contemplation proper. I would like, first of all, to quickly recapitulate what I was saying in part two. This will provide for us a good introduction to the topic at hand.

Recall that I mentioned that the kind of affective prayer experienced in the second stage, the coming to quiet—the quieting from external concerns that is so necessary for real prayer—is no longer so difficult to achieve. This second stage would in fact be when coming to quiet is easiest. It will become difficult once again, later in our prayer lives, but in this middle phase, quieting ourselves down, in terms of

preoccupations, outside distractions, is not so difficult because the heart is very much involved and
distractions don't bother us much.

When you are in a very emotional reunion scene
with one of your best friends, you usually don't have
to worry about distractions. If your emotions are very
much involved, all of you is caught up. This quieting
is the letting go of structures, the letting go of techniques, the letting go of all the ways that we attempt
to control the situation, all of the ways we try to
manipulate God. That's the type of quieting that
needs to happen here: quieting my instinct to control
things; quieting my desire for the familiar, my desire
to always trod the familiar paths and not to risk the
unknown. And I suggested that one way to let go of
these structures gracefully is to take the first ten or
fifteen minutes of the prayer and say to the Lord,
"Okay, you do whatever you want during this time.
If nothing happens, if you leave me to my own
resources, then after the ten or fifteen minutes I will
get to work and reflect and use my structures and
techniques. But before that, I will just keep quiet for a
while and give you a chance to take over if you
wish." That way I'm not forcing God, but I'm not
blocking God either. I think this can work quite well.

I also mentioned earlier that at this point, our
relationship to scripture changes and deepens.
Scripture, at this stage, is not simply the subject matter of our rational reflection, not just the object of our
consideration in prayer. At this stage, it is used more

to create the mood. If you recall, I used the example of the difference between getting information about my father, having my mother tell me familiar things about him, and actually encountering my father.

· When we go to scripture in the early stages of our prayer, we go for information about the Lord. By the later stages, we're quite familiar with scripture. There may be some new information encountered, but not much. As we pray and attend the liturgy, most of it will be more and more familiar to us, so that what happens is that what we hear in the scripture is not so much new insight—although that may continue to happen as we grow—but, rather, something echoing in our own heart, evoking a memory. Scripture becomes something we already know, and the heart is moved to love by recalling, just as with my father. My heart is moved to love by recalling the good things I know about him. So too, our hearts are moved to love the Lord by listening to the evangelists tell of things about God which we already know, which at this stage are not new, so that our use of the scripture is not so meditative or contemplative in the earlier sense, but it's more an exercise in remembering.

In order to transition to our final topic, I now wish to call attention to a subject I discuss in chapter 5 of *Opening to God*: The Active Purification of the Soul. In a sense, what happens in the third stage of growth is a carryover and a deepening of the earlier stages, and in this regard purification becomes the most important element to our prayer lives, perhaps for the rest of our lives. In heaven, of course, our prayer will be the vision of God, but I think here on earth it's much more the purifying transformation of ourselves, which for practically all of our lives on this earth I suspect, will be the major work of our prayer lives. This is the process of divinization.

Throughout the second, affective stage, purification becomes ever more important, because divinization begins in this life: we cannot become like God unless we are radically transformed. So, whereas we go to prayer to experience God in the second stage, gradually we begin to realize that the experience is in fact transforming us, that we are different in our encounters with people, that we're different in our work, that somehow the experience of God is not just a nice experience, but it is something transforming, something remaking us. Because of this purification, prayer at this time is very different from the first stage. Now it is much more the Lord's work and much less my work. Penance, the examen, the Sacrament of Reconciliation—these activities that are so essential to the first stage—will by necessity look different in the third stage. I think we can illustrate well what I mean by referring again for just a moment to the spiritual exercises of St. Ignatius.

To return to the analogy I used to describe the dynamics of the spiritual exercises, the contrast between the first week and the second week is like the contrast between emptying out the pot of exhausted dirt and dead weeds and roots, and filling the pot with new life. The first week is the emptying out of self in order that in the second week we can be filled with Christ. Now, the way most people make the first week of the retreat, the way most people make their examination of conscience, and the way most people make their confession is to evaluate themselves according to what they know of God's law, of God's obligation.

We know the scriptures and we ask, "How have I been doing that?" We know our catechism, we know the moral theology we've learned in whatever form we've gotten it, whether deep or elementary, and we know what we're supposed to do. We then check ourselves against this standard and either go to confession or make our examination of conscience and evaluate ourselves.

Notice that at this early stage, it is us doing the evaluating. You can perhaps see here where there is going to be a shift. What if I were to find out how God actually sees me instead of how I think God sees me? That might be very different. When I give retreats to people who are a bit more spiritually mature, I suggest that the grace of the first week is not properly sorrow for sin, because seeing it that way can be too active and too manipulative, in the sense that we have predetermined what should happen. I should feel sorrow. I should cry three quarts of tears. Only then am I ready to finish the first week.

And so I labor to cry, peeling onions and so on, to make sure that I accomplish my job for the first week.

Suppose that, instead of thinking that my job during the first week of the exercises was to produce some feeling, I instead saw my job was to see myself as God sees me; my job in the examination of conscience each evening would not be to evaluate myself, but to discover how the Lord saw my day. This might be very different from how I saw the day. When people I guide in the retreat agree to do this in the first week, I usually suggest to them that they first make a sort of profile of themselves. That part is not too difficult. Sometimes it's surprising what we find, but more often it is not—it is our own thinking about ourselves after all. After they finish their profile, I ask them to bring it before the Lord and listen—to ask God whether they are seen the way they see themselves. Something like, "Okay, Lord, I think this is how you see me, but now I'll let you speak for yourself." Do we ever do that? I suspect even the most pious people never do.

One good test I've discovered is this: I ask people who take prayer seriously, who confess regularly, if in all the many, many times they've confessed in their lives (it may be hundreds of times) have they ever asked what God wanted them to confess? Now, unless I have asked a very extraordinary person, the answer is usually no. Judging from others whom I've asked, people tend to say, "No, I never thought of it." When we go to confession, we tend to evaluate ourselves according to God's law—but it's my judgment. How different it might be if I said to the Lord, "Lord, today I'll have the opportunity to go to confession. What would you like me to confess? I'll be glad to confess—I can think of many things, and I'll be glad to confess any of them, but what really do you see as most in need of confessing? What do you see as most in need of healing?" We might be very, very surprised if we started confessing that way.

The first thing we might find out is that we're not quite sure how to tell what God might like. That means that we're not very good listeners. And that in turn means that we've probably been talking to God, not listening, all our lives, and we probably don't even know what accent God speaks with, whether Filipino or American, because we may never have heard God talk. It might be quite a salutary shock to discover that I haven't been very much of a listener because it's never even occurred to me to ask what God might like me to confess.

So I think there is a move between activity and receptivity, a move from talking to listening, and that move involves purification. The real heart of the matter is purification, or *purifying transformation*, to put it more positively. Purification is the negative aspect. Emptying out the pot. Transformation is the positive aspect, opening the pot to be filled by new life. They go together.

CONTEMPLATION:
DIVINIZATION

Throughout this work, I have been discussing three stages of growth. I have talked about knowing God, experiencing God, and then finally being transformed by God. It's that third stage which I would now like to explore in more detail. It's the stage of going from loving (the experiential and affective) to truly loving (contemplation). This stage can also be called transformation, or divinization. We become God. Jesus quotes at one point a verse from the Old Testament, "Do you not know that you are gods?" which is an extraordinary line. We've already seen something comparable in the third chapter of John's First Epistle: "We know this, that we shall be like him, that we shall know him as he knows us and as he knows himself." So the divinization which is our vocation is something which is almost beyond our comprehension or imagination.

I've spoken of the goal of our lives—being transformed, being divinized—as the positive dimension of purification in *When the Well Runs Dry*. In that book I describe divinization, which forms the third stage in a good prayer life as I see it, as "from loving to truly loving." Now, if we were to explain that distinction more fully and more thoroughly than I did in *Well* (and as I have reflected on it since), I would say that it's the difference between a deep, mature love, and a man and woman who marry at age twenty-five and say to one another, "I want to marry you because you fulfill all my desires."

To say with honesty, "I want to marry you because you fulfill all my desires" is not necessarily problematic. It can be a sign of real growth. Typically, the young person, before falling in love, is still quite centered on self. Most young people likely live under the assumption, "I don't need anybody else because I can fulfill myself." The boy who meets the girl and falls in love with her and discovers (as hopefully she discovers also), that neither he nor she can be sufficient unto themselves. They themselves are not enough for their own happiness—happiness has to come from someone else. I have to go out of myself, to stand outside of myself (which is what ecstasy means). I cannot find my fulfillment contained and enclosed within myself. I can only find it by going out to another. That is real growth from egocentrism to centering on someone else. But notice, it's not yet the fullness of growth.

"I love you because you fulfill all of my desires" is still essentially self-centered, isn't it? That's the way the young man is with the young woman at age twenty-five. And that's the way pray-ers are when they are twenty-five, also! "I love God because God fulfills me. I want to be a Carmelite contemplative because I find it so fulfilling to be praying all day." All right, that's growth. "I find that I cannot fulfill myself, that I need God to fulfill me." This is good, but it is not full maturity because it is still basically self-centered. A young man who says to his bride on their wedding day, at age twenty-five, "I love you because you fulfill all of my desires"—I think that's fine, very solid, in fact. But if a man says that to his wife on their golden wedding anniversary, I think something has gone very wrong.

Love is growth, and what is solid and appropriate at age twenty-five is not appropriate at age seventy-five. There should be maturing. Whereas the young man can say "I love you because you fulfill me," what the man should be saying at age seventy-five is, "I love you and therefore your fulfillment is my happiness. My love means that your joy is my joy." In other words, it's ecstatic in a double sense, that not only do I have to go out of myself to find my happiness, but I have to find my happiness precisely by forgetting it and thinking about the happiness of someone else. So that's the kind of transformation the Lord works in us, that we move from loving to truly loving, we move from finding joy in God to giving God joy.

The whole third stage is meant to bring us from a spirituality which is affective but essentially still self-centered (although we don't realize it when we are young) to a spirituality which is affective but much more other-centered. Such a spirituality, although it is affective (that is, it's of the heart), may not involve the emotions very much, and that can be very puzzling to people. Why? Because the emotions by their very nature are appetites. I'm not a psychologist, but as I understand it, our emotions are never truly altruistic. They don't give; they only take. Just like nobody has a generous stomach, so nobody has generous emotions. Those organs are not giving organs, they're taking organs. And our emotions by their very nature, like our stomach, devour whatever they desire. They don't give; they take.

Even our more altruistic emotions—if we can speak about them that way—will be, at the level of emotion alone, in some ways self-seeking. "I serve you because I find satisfaction in serving or because of the praise that I get or because it makes me feel self-righteous." Whatever the reasons may be, if the primary concern is feeling or emotion, there's going to be a good bit of the self there. That's precisely what the Lord has to purify within us, that centering on self in our love. It has to be transformed into a going out of ourselves, like the couple who are married fifty years, who don't think of themselves and their own happiness because each of them is totally concerned about the happiness of the other (those marriages are rare, but that's a really successful marriage). And their whole concern is not finding their own happiness, but giving happiness to someone else.

That's precisely the purpose of this third stage. Perhaps I should finish the thought by noting that if we think of the first stage as lasting perhaps one or two years in a good prayer life, and the second stage maybe lasting three or four (or maybe five) years, the third stage will probably last about fifty years! So even in terms of time, it's by far the dominant one for those who are faithful to prayer.

AT HOME IN THE
DARK

Unfortunately, many people spend fifty years in the second stage. Some people even spend fifty years in the first stage, not because it's a good thing but because they get stuck. But if we grow, no matter how well or how fast we grow, we're going to spend a long time in that third stage, the reason being that we're not naturally unselfish.

If you recall, what we are talking about is the move from loving to truly loving, that is, from loving in the sense of "you fulfill me" to truly loving in the sense of "my real joy is to fulfill you." As I said, that process is likely to take about fifty years, if we live that long. When people say to me, "How long is dryness in my prayer life going to last?" I always ask them, "How long do you plan to live?" because that's the only way I think we can answer that question.

It's important here to stress that while we are growing in the third stage, spiritual dryness should not necessarily be disturbing. Nor should spiritual darkness. One can learn to be at home in the dark. You can learn to be comfortable in the dark. You can go into the chapel in the evening when it's all very dark and find yourself, at first, very insecure because you can't see the benches. You don't know where anybody is. But after you've been in there a little while, you see quite well and your eyes adjust to the dark, and you can be at home there. You even find yourself thinking that it was strange that before you I felt very insecure. After a few minutes, it's as if you can see everything.

So, too, I think, with spiritual darkness, or dryness. We can become at home in it. Not after a few minutes, but after some time, and with good direction, which becomes more and more important here because at this stage in our prayer lives up is down and black is white and everything is the inverse of what we expect. So we will not be very good directors for ourselves, and, although books and talks on prayer can help, normally there will also be the need for personalized direction, in which the director is like a diagnostician, a doctor who can read the symptoms and check the signs and interpret for us what is really happening.

To do a bit of spiritual direction here (insomuch as we can), as our prayer moves from loving to truly loving, as we're being led through fifty years of growth from seeking our own fulfillment to truly loving in the sense of seeking to give God joy, what happens during that time is that God is the one who has to do this work in us. It's impossible for us alone. One of the things I notice with my young seminarians and the young sisters is that young people who are generous and eager to grow can sometimes be too eager. They can try to jump ahead of God. That's not a good idea.

This is my problem with some of the great Eastern traditions and some of the modern practices, where you learn to empty your head and so on, to just be blank. That's very dangerous, I think, because you're jumping ahead of God. Don't make yourself blank until God does it. And when God does it, don't fight it. That's the secret. In other words, let God be the boss. Don't empty your head. All of the great masters of prayer, who knew nothing about Zen or yoga, and all the great Christian masters in the West, all of them insist that we should continue meditating as long as we're able; that is, we should continue to be active until the Lord takes over. At the same time, once God takes over, we should not resist—although most of us will fight the process because it's strange to us and we don't know what to do.

You don't jump into the water and just let yourself sink, waiting for God to hold you up. No, as long

MEETING GOD
FACE TO FACE

N ow, when God does take over, that means that God is choosing to encounter us directly—not through images, but face-to-face. It's precisely the difference between knowing someone through pictures or through reading, and knowing the same person through meeting them. As long as you know them through images, that's like meditation or contemplation in the Ignatian sense—it's more imaginative reflection. You're knowing them indirectly through your faculties. This is contemplation in the sense of St. John of the Cross or Teresa. This is when we begin to encounter God directly, when God chooses to meet us directly and not just through our images, ideas, the parables of the gospel, and all the other things through which we can indirectly meet him: persons, sunsets, etc.

The time comes when God wants direct encounter with us, to meet us face-to-face. The difficulty is that God is infinite, but our faculties are not. Our faculties are finite. Therefore, they cannot encounter God directly. Our understanding can only grasp the finite. Our imagination can only grasp finite images. So when God meets us directly, the fuse in the circuit is rather overloaded, and we blow a fuse. That's why when God begins to meet the soul directly, we blank out because we can't grasp the infinite.

It's like St. Augustine said about encountering God, "It's like trying to put the ocean in a glass of water—a water glass. To try to pour the whole ocean into the glass." The glass is going to break. It simply cannot contain God. God is the ocean and our mind is the water glass. There's no way you can fit it in. And when the Lord starts to begin to encounter us directly, our faculties, our imagination, our understanding, our senses, they break down. And that's why we speak about the dark night or the dry well or the cloud of unknowing or the prayer of faith. All of those terms are really referring to the time where God begins to encounter the soul directly, and our faculties, being finite, cannot contain the infinite God. There's only one exception to this—the will.

The will is the only human faculty that is infinite, at least potentially. And as St. Augustine says very beautifully in one of the readings in the Liturgy of the Hours, "The whole of our life is God stretching the will until it is wide enough to contain the infinite." So when he encounters us directly, the union is between God and the will. The will is the only faculty that can somehow grasp the infinity of God, and therefore the other faculties, the imagination, the understanding, the senses, they become useless, as it were. They're of no help, and that's why prayer can seem very dry and very empty.

God encounters mature pray-ers no longer through images or pictures, which they can grasp, but in direct encounter, which they cannot grasp, so that the real union is between God and the will. That is why I stressed in chapter 1 of *When the Well Runs Dry* that St. Teresa's point about distractions is very, very important. Once our prayer becomes more like this, more contemplation in this sense, our attention is critical, but what we are to do in the face of distractions is somewhat surprising.

The word *contemplation* is an extraordinarily confused term in the history of spirituality. There are so many different uses of it that you can get lost. Here is how I define it—this is a valid use, and it's not an unusual one. I understand contemplation in the more passive sense, which I think is what St. John of the Cross means. Contemplation is when God takes over. God begins to encounter us directly and takes over the whole operation. Therefore, when our own faculties break down and are no longer of much help in prayer (which is why John calls it a dark night, because we're no longer able to work solely within our understanding and imagination) it paradoxically seems that God is absent. Why does God seem absent? Because we're used to images and ideas and they no longer work. We don't have them. And since that's the only thing we're used to, we think that we have lost God. And that's why good direction is extremely important. Because at the beginning of this stage, we could never judge for ourselves what was happening.

BECOMING ADULTS:
THE WILL

T o explain a bit further an image I used in *Well*, I mentioned there that, as we grow, prayer moves from the head in the first phase to the feelings in the second phase. Now in the third phase, prayer is more centrally located in the will. In this third stage, the feelings and the head seem blank or empty. Various things may happen to them during that time, and to help the pray-er understand what can occur in the mind and heart at this stage I like to use the image of children at an adult party. St. Teresa uses the image of doves, but, since I don't know much about doves, I didn't find that image very helpful. I suspect most people today don't know very much about doves either, whereas probably all of us know something about children. So I use the image of an adult party, which perhaps I can spell out a bit more.

When I was a youngster, I had a brother two years younger than me. My sister was a full twelve years younger, so my brother and I fought our way through childhood together. When my parents had visitors in the evening, the guests would come, and usually it was a little problematic. They wanted us to be seen by the guests, but they also wanted to be rid of us before we destroyed the party!

Normally what would happen was that the children would eat early, before the visitors came. My parents were simultaneously feeding the children and getting rid of them! Once we finished eating, we'd have to take a bath and put on our pajamas, and by then the guests would arrive. And when the guests arrived, we were allowed about twenty minutes to entertain the guests and be the life of the party and get all sorts of attention. When our twenty minutes were finished, we were sent off to bed so that the adults could talk to one another. If we were around, it would have been hopeless to talk.

In this analogy, the children are the understanding and the imagination, while the adults are God and our will. The understanding and the imagination don't grasp what's going on between the will and God, and because they don't grasp it they're like children at an adult party longing for attention. That's why we had to be put to bed when we were little, because if we stayed up it would have ruined the conversation of the adults.

What is happening between God and the will is largely meaningless to the understanding and imagination—they cannot grasp it. Therefore, they clamor for attention, and one of three things may happen to them: First, they may be put to "bed," as in my story of my own childhood. Now, when they're put to bed, it's rather nice in the sense that there's no disturbance. That's when people feel and say to me, "Father, I don't know whether I was asleep or awake. I sat down to pray and the next thing I knew, the prayer time was over. I was very peaceful. I had no thoughts in my head, but it went so fast that I have the feeling that I might have been sleeping, and yet I know I wasn't sleeping because I know where I was." What that means is that the Lord has put the understanding and the imagination to sleep. God put them to bed so they won't interfere with the work going on in the will.

Putting the understanding and the imagination "to sleep" happens, I think, more often at the beginnings of a more passive prayer life. But as with my example of how my parents dealt with my brother and myself, this cannot last. My parent's method of putting us to bed so that the adults could enjoy themselves and speak intelligibly to one another was effective when we children were four, five, or six.

However, the time came when my mother had to let us stay up. She couldn't be putting us to bed so early when we were thirteen and fifteen and seventeen and twenty. Sooner or later, we had to be allowed to stay awake, and that meant trouble, because it was much easier for her to put us to bed and get rid of us.

Why did she have to let us stay awake? Because we would never grow up unless we learned to handle ourselves with adults. And I think that the analogy works here with God. Gradually, God has to leave the understanding and the imagination awake, even though they are left out of what's really happening. God cannot keep putting them to sleep or else they will never grow. Now when God leaves them awake, like older children at an adult party, what they do, since what is happening between the adults still has little meaning to them, is that they tend to wander off by themselves; or they revert to clamoring for attention; or they may find ways to amuse themselves.

This is the second possibility. The first is that the Lord may put the imagination and understanding to sleep, in which case we just need to be reassured that we're not really negligent or insulting God, but that things are fine. In the second case, God may leave the understanding and the imagination awake, and then we will be filled with distractions.

This can be very frustrating, because it seems we're insulting God. But it's not so. No, the kids go off and amuse themselves when the adults' conversation has no meaning to them. That is why St. Teresa says that at this stage in our prayer lives it's far better to just ignore the distractions and not to fight them. Early in your prayer life, it's necessary to fight distractions because you're using your understanding and your imagination in your prayer, and you cannot think of two things at once. So you have to fight the distractions and strive to concentrate.

At this stage, though, if you fight the distractions, the will, which is united to the Lord, is continually being pulled away, like a mother who's always disciplining her kids while she has visitors. And there's no communication between her and the visitors because she's continually disciplining the kids.

Sometimes a mother may ignore her kids, and they become much better behaved. It can be a very good idea to ignore them, unless of course they start demolishing the house! Usually, though, the children clamor for attention, but mother ignores them and goes on with the adults, and what happens is that gradually the kids settle down and amuse themselves or become quiet. But if you keep disciplining them, then they know how to get attention, and so they will be more and more unruly. Mothers who are constantly disciplining their children usually have much more unruly children than mothers who know how to ignore them. The more attention the kids get, the more obnoxious they become, because they're seeking for attention and they've found out how to get it.

There is a third possibility. The third possibility is that sometimes what is happening between the Lord and the will may overflow into the understanding. Sometimes the children may hear the adults talk about something, for example, about their schoolteacher, which is very fascinating for them. For a few moments the conversation has meaning to them. And unfortunately they hear things you didn't want them to hear when you thought they were not listening. Sometimes what is happening between the Lord and the will overflows into the understanding and the imagination, and there will be consolation—there will be a great sense of God in the feelings and the understanding, the imagination, the senses. But that overflow is very secondary. It's what we tend to think of as the heart of our prayer, and it's what we tend to seek. But in truth, that is not the heart of prayer. What is primary in the prayer is that the Lord is working in the will. Gradually, through the will, God will transform and divinize the other faculties, too.

CONCLUSION

In conclusion, how can we briefly indicate the effect this third stage has on the other stages? We mentioned earlier that the stages are not in fact clearly delineated, but rather they flow one into the other. To begin, I think we could say that quiet is not as much a problem at this point, once the prayer becomes very dry. It's not so difficult to come to quiet; in fact, it's almost automatic that we can move into the quiet quickly and easily, and that's a very good sign. We need good signs at this point, because people tend to be discouraged by the dryness and the seeming absence of God. So, one very good sign that you'll normally find is that it's quite easy to come to quiet. Secondly, even though my prayer is very blank, I think that it will be true that we won't have much problem staying awake.

Earlier, when we first began to move into the blankness, we may have found ourselves easily falling asleep because our faculties were bored, and people normally fall asleep when they're bored. I always tell them, don't worry about it; just sleep and pray when you wake up, because you'll do more harm by fighting it. But after a while, soon enough, you'll find that you don't sleep. The sleep comes primarily from the boredom, and I think the important thing is just to ride through that boredom and get used to the blankness so that you're not bored by it. But that will only happen by letting it be. So I say, if you do sleep, sleep, and pray when you wake up, and you'll find as you go along that strangely enough, even though nothing is happening, you won't sleep, and that won't be a problem.

As you might expect, our growth at this stage becomes almost entirely God's work. At this point, there's practically nothing we can do about it. Penance as an activity in our lives becomes much less important, I think. It always has value, but more and more, the penances in our lives that are important are the ones the Lord sends. And rest assured, God will send plenty. Normally at this stage, we won't have to go looking for penance because there will be plenty built right into our lives.

For example, in prayer, one of the great penances will be learning, gracefully, to do nothing. That alone will take a good bit of one's energy. Then there is the penance of being flexible, of learning to live without structures, of learning to be in the sea of God without a life raft. See, all life rafts are an obstacle here. If we need them, fine. If we're too insecure to be without them, fine. But you can't learn to float in God as long as you're hanging on to a life raft.

Growth is frequently blocked by all of the structures, all of the security blankets, all of the familiar patterns of prayer and so on. Everything we hold on to restricts our flexibility and limits what God can do. And that will be a very great penance because all of us by nature seek security. To let go of those things will be costly. Thirdly, I think a very big penance in the area of prayer is resisting the temptation to evaluate what is happening, to try to get reassurance every two days that I'm really on the right track, to continually be anxious. I think we eventually come to the point where we find ourselves saying to the Lord, "If I'm wrong, and if I go to hell, okay; it was out of love; it's your problem, not mine. I did what I thought was best, and I don't believe anybody could be lost for doing that." And beyond that, I don't worry about it.

Learning not to worry is essential, because our anxieties really do block our growth. I've been talking up to now about darkness in our prayer, but the main darkness really is the "darkness in the marketplace," which means our lives with others. This darkness can become the real penance of our lives. What is happening within prayer happens outside as well, and what is happening with God happens with people. Sometimes growth is painful because whereas God loves our growth, sometimes people are threatened by it. The very same growth in Jesus which pleased the Father angered the Pharisees, not because Jesus was different in his way of behaving, but because they were different in their way of reacting.

At this point, the whole of our prayer becomes the writing of the fifth gospel, the gospel that we write in our own lives. And the evangelists become at this point not guides or teachers but rather companions on the journey. It's at this time, I think, that St. John the Baptist becomes a very real figure in our lives, and it's at this time that Paul comes alive for us. Paul is hard for beginners, because he presupposes the gospel. Paul is very subjective. The question that Paul is answering in his letters is not "who is Jesus Christ?" which is the question of the gospels but, rather, who is Jesus Christ for me? That is a very subjective question, and it becomes a very real, very alive question for us once we have ourselves come to know the Lord. Paul's words will then echo our own experience, and what before seemed very heavy and difficult to grasp becomes very real.

Finally, as we grow, our taste in scripture changes and we find ourselves valuing parts of scripture that before we found not so appealing. Chapters 5, 7, and 8 of the Gospel according to St. John are good examples for me. These are chapters I found to be among the last ones I came to like. And yet I would say now that I find them the deepest, the most valuable, because of the radical singleness of Jesus' love there—his passion for the Father, for example. Those chapters are rather austere in their single-mindedness, like John the Baptist as a person. But as you grow, you begin to desire more of that directness, and less of the beating around the bush in more indirect ways of talking.

To end, I leave you with the question, "How do I name God?" If we call God "beloved," that implies several things. Naming God "beloved" is the goal of our lives (and that's what this whole process is leading to). Doing so implies, first of all, that God and I have been through much together. Secondly, it implies that we can be totally free with each other, that I can speak to God with total frankness. Thirdly, it implies that I am totally centered on God. And once we begin to value being loving more than being holy, we can then say we have begun the experience of a real relationship—one of giving God joy rather than getting something for myself.

THOMAS H. GREEN, S.J., (1932–2009) was an internationally recognized teacher, mentor, and author, best known for his classic works on prayer, including *Opening to God, When the Well Runs Dry,* and *Weeds Among the Wheat.* Fr. Green served as the Spiritual Director of San Jose Seminary, Manila, Philippines, and Professor of Philosophy and Theology at Ateneo de Manila University.

Founded in 1865, Ave Maria Press,
a ministry of the Congregation of
Holy Cross, is a Catholic publishing
company that serves the spiritual and
formative needs of the Church and its
schools, institutions, and ministers;
Christian individuals and families; and
others seeking spiritual nourishment.

For a complete listing of titles from

Ave Maria Press

Sorin Books

Forest of Peace

Christian Classics

visit www.avemariapress.com

 ave maria press / Notre Dame, IN 46556
A Ministry of the Indiana Province of Holy Cross